CW00419584

ECHO
THE
SILENCE

ECHOING
THE
SILENCE

John Skinner

GRACEWING

First published in 2009

Gracewing
2 Southern Avenue, Leominster
Herefordshire HR6 0QF

All rights reserved. No part of this publication may be reproduced, stored in a retrieval system, or transmitted in any form, or
by any means, electronic, mechanical, photocopying, recording or
otherwise, without the written permission of the publisher.

© John Skinner 2009

The right of John Skinner to be identified as the author of this
work has been asserted in accordance with the Copyright,
Designs and Patents Act 1988.

ISBN 978 0 85244 193 0

Illustrations by Reynolds Stone.
Originally published in *Reynolds Stone Engravings* (John Murray 1977),
reproduced by kind permission of Phillida Gili.

Typeset by Action Publishing Technology Ltd,
Gloucester GL1 5SR

CONTENTS

v

PROLOGUE

'Be silent before the Lord.' Zeph. 1:7

Instinctively we fall silent before the truly beautiful, good and awesome. Words can bring us to the threshold, they cannot enter in. The best of adoration is silent.

The texts gathered in this book are but humble signs that invite to awareness of something beyond the immediately given, day by day. Nobody has ever heard silence. No one has ever seen the Father. Yet he who has seen me has seen the Father. Christ and all creation is the sacrament of the Father.

We cannot hear silence but we can catch some echo of its passage if we are attentive with a simple receptive listening, receiving and acquiescing to what cannot be named and from which come all names, fragile moments of reflected beauty and fleeting glory.

All sound is born of silence and ultimately returns to its embrace and its fullness.

God is love. I go to the Father, for he is greater than I.

Peace and Joy, in Xt Fr Cyril Pierce

INTRODUCTION

I have been encouraged to put together a second book of readings and reflection on silent prayer by the warm reception the first has received. My publisher Tom Longford, and all his staff at Gracewing, must be thanked: I have had more letters and contacts from this little book than from any previous title of mine. Some have come from distant parts – The Philippines and South America – some have led to on-going contacts, all confirm that many more people take their interior prayer seriously than at first meets the eye.

Once again, I must thank my friends the Carthusians of Parkminster for their continuing support of *Hear our Silence*. What began as a straightforward book describing my stay with them a decade ago soon grew into an open invitation for all to listen to the Silence within. And so our workshops continue, when we come together to experience and explore the prayer of silence; and I give details of how to contact me at the back of this book. So too does our circle of friends grow – people who support our initiative and who receive my monthly letter and four readings.

It is from these readings that the present book flows. What is there to say about silent prayer, some might ask. I reply, a very great deal by any number of witnesses spread across the centuries and lapping into our present hectic and noisy world. It is only by sharing our common experience that we grow in prayer, that is to say become more familiar with the relationship of Divine Love which is this great gift from within.

John Skinner

JANUARY

JANUARY
the way ahead

Once again, I stand at the head of a New Year: or do I look back at the year just passed, with all its companion years jostling and jeering over its shoulder. My rank of years do not seem to stack up too much. Or so it seems in human terms.

It will always be so, if we look through human eyes. But if we turn our telescope the right way round, we may perhaps begin to see human life from our Maker's perspective. The whole point of living is that it never adds up. That is precisely its purpose. Life is all about change not achievement.

'I am the Way', you tell me. And did your life stack up, achieve, end well and with fine purpose. Or was it not a terrible, mysterious unravelling that had your enemies quietly satisfied that a problem had been put to rest.

And as they washed their hands and went home to their beds, your friends wept at the misery of it all.

'I am the Way': the only way. This is the way: it will never be your way, your idea of how things should turn out. Follow my way and you will see the similarities in your life to my own. For I am asking you to allow me to show you the way, the best way. Not the perfect way, the path you would necessarily choose to follow, but my way. This way.

So this is the life you have given me: you have offered me none other. I will accept this life and all that I have and have not made of it. Yet there I go again. I do not make my life: you fashion it with me and in me. This is the New Year change I seek. As John said: 'He must grow greater: I must grow smaller.'

Each new day in this year, each new moment of every day let me follow your way. 'Lord, to whom else can we go: you have the message of Life. You are our Way.'

the way ahead

Another year
the way ahead seems endless
considering how far I've come

I look back
on all those years passed
yet
I have barely begun

Stuck in treacle
trapped in time
life like sand betwcen my fingers
slips away

Another year
to make new way
your Way

'I am the Way'
you say

Be my Way
each new day
this year

JOHN SKINNER

echoes of Silence

I was brought to Silence ten years ago when I first met the English Carthusians. Their entire life is shaped by silence and solitude in a monastic tradition that stretches back 900 years. Here a Carthusian meditates on the quality of true Silence.

First notice how he distinguishes human silence, silence of our own making, with Silence itself. True Silence is the Silence of encounter when we are aware of the mystery of our being shaped by our Maker in his own image. A process, never a fixed point. How our very existence is part of the mystery of creation in time, the outpouring of God's inner Love from within the timeless Trinity. For the Father utters us through his Word in Love. As he continually breathes life into us, enabling us to be who we are, he does so in Love. For this is the only way he can be, the sole manner in which he acts. And we depend upon him for every breath we breathe, as we collaborate with the work of our be-coming – a process, never a fixed point.

In our silent, receptive prayer we try to contemplate this amazing mystery. And as we still our inner thoughts, reaching to the seat of the soul, the ground of our being, we come to the gift of Silence. It is as if our breath had been knocked out of us: now given back once more. We are still, at peace, finally at rest.

Words fade. For words are useless here. We gaze into the Silence believing 'it is Thou'. We hear the reply 'I it am'. The mystery remains. All we can do is hope in this Silence, trust and receive his gift of Love.

echoes of Silence

The silence you can utter
is not Silence itself

Our silence is a direct perception of mystery
a sort of experience of the immense reality
that enfolds and engenders us

For we too are part of it
we too are mystery opening onto unlimited horizons

The Unborn cannot be conceived
He stands at the door and knocks

We let him in
when we enter quietly into ourselves
to open our hearts and minds
to what is beyond our little objectified
constructed world and ego

We let him in
when we have to receive what is
without trying to grasp it
to be in trust
that all is gift
all finally love

Silence becomes the fullness of our fragmented words
an act of hope and faith
that beyond time and death
sin and suffering
all will be well
for all is well

God in himself
and we and all things in him
is Love

A CARTHUSIAN

I it am

This mantra-like saying is one of the cornerstones of the simple message of Julian of Norwich – how the loving Trinity touches us intimately every moment of our lives. And it is the cornerstone of our prayer of silence: we must believe and trust as we pray that God wants our prayer of attention infinitely more than ever we do as we set out to pray.

The refrain 'I it am' carries overtones of Yahweh's utterance to Moses in Exodus. 'Who shall I say that sent me: they will ask me for your name . . .?' And the response: 'I am who I am: say to the sons of Israel, I am has sent me – this is my name for all time.'

I hear God telling Moses, don't let my people ask silly questions. If I were to answer that question, you would never begin to understand. Just take me for who I am: the Other who gives life, who loves, who is with you.

As we pray, we must know, in faith and hope, that 'the God of our fathers, the God of Abraham, the God of Isaac, the God of Jacob' is with us, filling our individual and unique person with his Love.

Julian certainly experienced this time and again: and her amazingly confident message of love repeats it again and again. Moreover, she is convinced that her long life of solitude in her Norwich anchorhold, while she pondered her sixteen showings and recorded their meaning of Love, was not for her alone: 'but these were shown to me and all my even Christians'.

'I it am that you love, whom you desire.' Too often, as we allow ourselves to be swamped by our failings, we neglect the central truth: that all our working in this life is both from above and centred within. Of ourselves, we may do nothing: yet all is already accomplished. All we have to do is to receive.

'I it am that is all: I it am that showed myself: shows myself to you – here.'

I it am

I it am

I it am

I it am that you love

I it am that you like

I it am that you serve

I it am that you long for

I it am that you desire

I it am that you mean

I it am that is all

I it am that shows myself

to you

here

JULIAN OF NORWICH
The Twelfth Showing

on this Way we need no sandals

Origen was one of the earliest Fathers whose influence on the patristic tradition is hard to exaggerate. In the early days, Christians were still awakening to the new reality and understanding of the person and power of Christ. Questions were continually asked and answers given by the likes of Origen. He was a gifted teacher who took over the catechetical school of Alexandria at the age of seventeen, just two hundred years after the birth of Jesus. It was his gifted insights about the mystery of Christ's life and death that laid the foundation of much that was to follow. In particular, he stressed that the Christian way is directly linked in a continuous path through the Jewish experience of God's revelation of himself contained in the Old Testament; for this leads in to God's explicit utterance of the Word, Jesus the Son of Man, appearing, teaching and enacting in his own life and death the solemnly promised relationship or covenant established long before.

Moses guided the People of God through the desert. Origen likewise encourages us on our journey: our way forward is twofold, achieved by word and by deed. We may seek the Truth in Christ's words, slowly growing in his wisdom. And as we do so, our response is signalled by our deeds of love. It is a simple Way but we must learn to travel light. 'We must take nothing with us . . . no cloak, no staff, no sandals.' This lyrical passage is typical of Origen's teaching; his theology is notable for its allegorical approach. He prefers symbols to concrete facts. For in our dealings with the mystery of living and growing and changing, there are no hard and fast signposts, no map to ensure we never stumble or lose our way. We must walk in faith, one step at a time, always knowing that, like the followers of Christ travelling to Emmaus, he will fall in step beside us: he will light us on our Way, for he is the only Way.

on this Way we need no sandals

We may understand
how Christ is the Way
if we consider
how we make progress in wisdom

We go forward
seeking Truth in the Divine speech
the Word
By our actions
we conform to goodness

We may take nothing with us
on this Way
neither bag nor cloak
we need no staff
no sandals for our feet

The Way alone
is enough
He will provide
all we need for our journey

For those who walk this Way
will lack nothing
They wear the guest-robe of one who is going to a wedding

They will meet no misfortune
on their Way

ORIGEN ON JOHN

FEBRUARY

FEBRUARY

being and becoming

I Am Who I Am, Moses was told as he encountered his Maker, mysteriously manifested in a bush that was on fire. We view Moses and other persons who speak to us of God as far apart from us, not just in time but in being. Yet we are all members of this sprawling human family sired by our One Maker, the Being who Is and pours his Living Spirit within us all.

Such is a noble challenge by Johannes Metz as he begins his little gem *Poverty of Spirit*. Written fifty years ago and still in print, it was loaned to me last year by my friend Michael, Bishop of Exeter. We were talking after Sunday Eucharist when he suddenly disappeared into his library and came back with Metz's slim red volume. 'Let me have it back,' was his plea. And you can see why.

I watched a recent Sunday night television programme entitled 'The meaning of life'. I should have known better than to stay up and watch. A range of well-known heads all had their sound bite say on what they thought about human existence. One mentioned love – 'like money, you should spend it, share it around'; another religion – 'tells us to save our living until after we are dead'. Neither very profound, but at least they were vaguely on song. As for the rest: they seemed like butterflies blown about in a gale.

Metz brings us to our senses in his opening paragraph. Life is about commerce with our Creator. Yes, money and love are analogous: but love far outstrips the former. And the intimate invitation underlying our being alive is to respond moment by moment to our relationship with our Maker. For the Father of our human family is no watchmaker who has fashioned a piece and laid it aside as finished: we are in our making on a daily, moment by moment relationship of love.

being and becoming

Becoming a human being
involves
more than conception and birth

It is a mandate
or command
a decision

To be human
means
an open-ended relationship
to oneself

I do not possess Being
my being is challenged continually
by the
Being
Who Is

I
within my Humanity
am
continually
challenged
questioned
from my depths
to fathom
to swim
to Be
within his Boundless Spirit

JOHANNES METZ
Poverty of Spirit

13

Christ – God's seed in us

Fearful of God's true intimacy with us, we prefer to keep him at arm's length. Irenæus, Bishop of Lyons a mere century after the death of Christ, will have none of this. He came to Gaul from Smyrna where as a boy he listened to the preaching of Bishop Polycarp. Now he himself was a disciple of John which explains the familiarity with this powerful imagery of the Son being uttered to mankind as Word.

This direct line of teaching shines out in his opening paragraph where Irenæus delights in compressing John's insight into God's loving intimacy both within himself and without as he extends his loving self-knowledge to include the whole of creation. As the Father eternally generates his Son who is his image and equal, so through his Son he speaks aloud. The least created being, the smallest star or grain of sand, is uttered in his Word. His stamp or image permeates all creation. But since the Word has not stinted but flowed into mankind in the Person of Jesus, this same seal, image – divine seed – is at the root of our being. We may not escape this relationship of overflowing love, however we might seek to ignore it.

Bridging this mysterious gulf between the eternal perfection of the One Being and the sprawling, apparent chaos of creation is the task of Christ as he invites us to join him in his overall plan: to shape and re-order all that he has made. As my eyes are opened and I open my heart and purpose to him, so I grow more like the divinized being he lovingly intends me to become.

We are all in our making.

In the work of his passion, death and rising, Christ has passed his power of Love, which is knowledge of the nature of his Father, over to us. One day, all will be fulfilled, all revealed: we will be dazzled by the majestic labour he has achieved. But for now we live in faith, as we receive the power of his loving grace. We know that we are continually uttered within the Loving Word as we are being incorporated in Christ: for he 'utters mankind in himself'.

And in so doing, he reveals the Father to his human family:
'He who is unseen, may now be seen.'

Christ – God's seed in us

The Word
only Son of the Father
is ever present to mankind
He is at one with the work
that he has fashioned in his Father's knowledge
for he has impregnated it
with his own divine seed (1 Jn 3:9)

He has suffered for us
he has risen again for us
he will come once more
in the glory of the Father
to raise all Flesh

Then he will reveal
the work of his salvation
to dazzle the universe

There is but one God
one only Father
one only Christ
who is Jesus our Lord
He utters the universe in himself
within this universe
there is mankind –
Being made by God
thus Christ utters mankind
in himself

It is for this
He who is unseen
may now be seen

St Irenæus
(*c.* AD 130–200)

15

'I saw God in a point', declares Julian as challenging as ever Eckhart can be. It is a wonderful metaphor to play with. Seeing the point of God, realizing that God has a point: that God is so simple, so ineffable that he is best represented by the infinity of a single point.

I once had a Jesuit schoolmaster, Willy Wetz, who was a wizard teacher of maths. When it came to geometry, he would begin his first lesson by fashioning a perfect circle on the blackboard – freehand. It was a wonderful trick: we all fell silent at his mastery. Eckhart joins in the geometry play.

Eckhart sees God drawing his perfect circle in which we and all creation are enclosed. It is as if God's womb enfolds the created universe – which is still being fashioned. Julian assures us that 'God is nearer to us than our own soul'. And here he is steadily, lovingly at work.

In the words of the psalmist, 'we are being knitted', made whole. His work is unfinished still: and we must assist him in his task.

'Deep within our soul, God is making his Universe – of which we are an integral point – whole once more.'

making his universe whole

I saw God in a point

Being is his circle
in this circle
at this point
all creatures exist

All that is in God
is God

I have often told you
God is creating the whole universe
he is making it
fully and wholly
now
all at once

God is nearer to us
than our own soul

He is nowhere nearer
than in our soul
Here
where there is no time
no image may come
deep within our soul
God is making his universe whole

JOHN SKINNER
(based on Julian, Eckhart)

as I am loving you

Christ's final words to his friends as they sat together sharing their last meal was about love. 'You must love each other – in the same way as I have always loved you.' And in the following twenty-four hours leading up to his cruel dying he poured out his love upon them, enacting his own words.

His message, the very reason for his existence as Man among men – Son of Man, as he continually named himself – was to give back true love to his human family, his own life blood transfused into human stock. So that now our human love may be transformed into true self-giving. The very Love by which the Father knows his Son, the same love by which he speaks his Word into our hearts, is given to us in the Spirit of Jesus' own love for us. The circuit of Divine Loving – an intimacy which we cannot as yet glimpse but merely name as 'the Trinity' – breaks into our everyday human affairs. We are called simply to receive the power of his own loving, to accept the one gift he came to offer us. The power of love – the gift of himself, Jesus, the Son of Man – is present to us.

This power of his Love we receive as we pray. We enact it, as he did, in all our human relationships. And so the dead Christ is risen in us as we become dead to ourselves and he lives again in our love.

as I am loving you

Love
one another
as I
have loved you

I know all about love
its delights
and dangers

I long to love
deeply
and in truth

Sounding the deep silence
of human love
to come to
Love itself

To receive Love
so as to share Life

Your very own Working
'As I am Loving You'

JOHN SKINNER

MARCH

MARCH

miserere

Lent comes round again: how will I use the opportunity this time in a positive way? First, I must face up to myself – the real me, not my camouflaged image hiding in self-deception. And that is all said in the great psalm of repentance which was wrung from David's heart when he knew the extent of his separation from his Maker.

Contrition is opening my inner self to the true score without concealment. Yet that may perhaps only be possible if I am able to trust in the absolute and unconditional forgiveness of my Father. He has been waiting for me to return home for a long time. While I am still a long way off, he hastens to greet me. I must open my heart and recognize all that separates us: once done, the debris becomes dust. The rest is his gift.

The gift of a new beginning, a fresh start, a new heart – into which he pours his Spirit of Love: all is his working. What I need to do is to turn on my heel to leave my muddle, my mess and start the journey home. It is a journey which will last my whole life-time. Yet it is a journey full of hope and faith. A walk sometimes in the darkness, but my passage is always lit by the sure knowledge that I will arrive at a place called home.

Note on 'the Father'
Many people I meet cannot accept the traditional biblical image of the Father as the root of the One God, the Begetter of Son and Spirit. I think this is due to their own bad experience of a father. Despite its origin on the lips of Jesus, Father – naming the One God – is still an image and metaphor. For there is no human name that utters God in his fullness. So that if 'Father' fails to speak, find another – friend, companion, lover, heart's desire, eternal one, Alpha.

Jesus constantly named a person to whom he related in a primary loving and devoted way. He called him Father. His friends understood and hungered to know that same friendship. 'Show us your Father,' Philip pleads. But Jesus tells him: 'To have seen me, is to have seen the Father.'

miserere

Have mercy on me
Lord of all goodness
Tenderest Father
wipe away my mistakes
wash away my sins
banish all my guilt

I come before you
fully aware of all that stands between us

Create a new heart within
Pour you Spirit anew
to refresh me in your joy

Open my lips
and my mouth will sing your praises

My only offering is this broken spirit
give me new heart
Fill it with your peace and love
only then
am I
pleasing to you

PSALM 52

Only after the great, individual journey, does every great mystic assert the unknown Otherness of God. Here, Rumi, the thirteenth-century Persian mystic poet, warns us not to know our Maker.

For if once we try to become familiar with God, name him, we tidy him away, keep him at arms length or 'in a box' of our own fashioning. So we diminish him, and eventually he will exist no more than a genie in our lamp which we polish at will so that he may appear for us to do our bidding. That is the danger: what the reality?

Have no fear: God *is* near. But there lies the problem. We sense his true reality only to take fright and flee. How may we stand our ground? Simply, by not trying to do but to receive. That is the true message of love. For the genuine Lover never seeks to invade or overwhelm, rather to enhance and enrich: and he is always present – Silently.

As a boy, my mother insisted on half an hour piano practice before I went into the field to fly my kite. I was forever looking over my shoulder at a poplar tree to judge the strength of the wind. Our wind is forever in our sails, if only we have faith and believe. 'Your faith has made you whole again,' his generous words. Notice, not 'I cured you with my superb power, how lucky you are ...' But crediting the person with their own cure, allowing them to own themselves once more.

This is the true humility of our Maker: he invites us to join his task as partners in our 'Again-Making'. Such was the vision of Julian of Norwich as she kept silently to her cell year by year, echoing the wisdom of an unknown companion pilgrim in distant Persia.

circle of Silence

God is near
God is far

God is wary
God is weary

God is tired of being called GOD
weary that I always avoid his Love
slip down the blind side
and call it something less

Let me not
cheapen your approaches

You have told me who you are

I am who I am

Your activity in my head
your hand around my heart
with this circling inside

root of my being

I cannot name
what circles
so perfectly

Only know
your Silence encircling me

JOHN SKINNER
(after Rumi)

poverty of spirit

'How happy are the poor in spirit,' your very opening words as you taught the crowds that followed you in their hunger. 'Blessed are you – for the Kingdom of heaven itself is yours.'

So this poverty is the key to your Kingdom. What is it to be poor, poor in spirit? It is none other than setting all things, all entanglements aside. Did you not say 'Foxes have their holes, birds too their nests – yet the Son of Man has nowhere to lay his head and rest.' You set us such high standards, you who came down from above to be among men. 'Son of Man' was your calling card: never Son of God.

And yet, am I not missing the point entirely: the Kingdom, which you would give me, is such a perfect and fulfilling gift that if I have anything less, it will pass me by. If I am not hungry, there is no appetite to sit at your table. If I cannot recognize you (as John did) at first sight, then I will pass you by and walk my own way – alone.

poverty of spirit

I am not he
said John

But John knew at once the Christ
as soon as he saw him
passing by

I too am not
am ignorant
empty of heart
poor of spirit
all this a preparation
a hunger
in order to encounter
You

Do not pass me by
open my eyes
like John
to see
my heart to hear

John told them
this is the One

Come and see
you said
I too hear
your silent invitation

JOHN SKINNER

27

our home of prayer

A word of introduction. In AD 246, Cyprian, like Augustine after him, became a Christian, resigning his office of rhetor. This Imperial official was an important public person charged with promoting Latin, the common language that maintained the Emperor's rule far and wide. So when Cyprian was baptized, he became a doubly marked man. Within two years, the Christians of Carthage voted him their bishop; and when a year later persecution broke out Cyprian had to flee the city.

Cyprian's invitation to prayer is stunning: 'in this home of his ...' What wonderful confidence, what familiarity: here is a guide we can follow. And yet he is echoing God's very own invitation, the living example of his servant Jesus who walked among men, sat down at table with his friends, taught and healed and loved all mankind. For prayer is our encounter with this very same Son of Man.

He it is 'who wants us to find peace, joined with one another, living in the same Spirit, his Spirit who bears his Love'. This is the simple reality of prayer: an intimate encounter with the Loving Trinity who invite us home. And in this home – which we share with the whole human family – we live a new life, the dynamic, living Love of God Our Father.

Cyprian reminds us that we were given this new life when we were plunged into the waters of our baptism, re-enacting the death and burial of Jesus, so that we might rise with him newly born. Each time we pray, we refer back to this mystery, for the Father continually gives us his Son just as Jesus breathes forth his Loving Spirit into our heart.

our home of prayer

In this home of his
which is prayer
God
wants us to find peace
joined with one another
living in the same Spirit
his Spirit
bearing his Love

He wants us
to live this new life
that we have been given
in baptism

We are now become
children of God

Let us live in his peace

We have been given
One Spirit

Let us have
one heart
and a single thought

The divine union
of the Trinity
Father
Son
and Holy Spirit
joins us together

SAINT CYPRIAN
(d. 258)

29

APRIL

APRIL

where do words come from?

Art invites us to be alive through our senses to our soul's inner awakening. The painter has visions of colour and form which he shares with us if we but look over his shoulder. The musician opens our ears to fresh and beguiling sounds which we have not heard before. The dancer demonstrates the joy of movement in praise of the body's intense beauty.

All art quickens the soul. But the simplest paving stones of art itself are words. This is how we communicate, this the magic of awakening. No wonder children's stories are full of spells and strange surprises fashioned from words.

And the true beauty of words is that I know not where they come from. Like some crystal-pure spring, words come to my lips as if from deep below: not of my making, but wondrous gifts seeking wisdom, showing my way ahead, offering the promise of companionship.

At least, that is how they ought to work. But humankind is so very good at wasting words, abusing speech, twisting meanings to suit foul ends. The pollution of words, spilling them without sense or reverence is my most grievous crime.

So that silence may perhaps be the antidote, the bridle of my tongue. Reflection too plays its part. If I dwell on meaning, seek truth, cultivate simplicity, then my words when uttered will be well: they will be fruitful, fulfil their purpose – which is to inform both myself and the person to whom I relate.

where do words come from?

Like light from above
like dew descending

Autumn leaves falling
salmon rising
frost crusting

Waves tumbling
surf spewing
water toppling
pebbles rumbling

Sun warming
lambs skipping
buds pushing
grass greening

Seeds starting
bees questing
flowers inviting
stones glowing

Spring again
Your Easter Gift

JOHN SKINNER

my Spirit of Truth is yours all ways

I go back again and again to those five key chapters of John, 13-17: Jesus' final words to his friends as he lovingly sums up his life's task. But before this intimate final scene, John tells of a terrifying altercation that took place publicly in The Temple. Hostile crowds gather as the Pharisees whip up hatred with their words. Jesus stands his ground and tells them the Truth about himself in fresh words they may not comprehend.

'When you have lifted up the Son of Man: you will know that I am he.'

How could they have made sense of so few words: expressing both prophecy and the whole Truth about this man standing before them. Reading them off the page today, with the gift of hindsight, these sayings are almost too powerful for our ears to hear. So best listen with heart.

The nature of this Son of Man, it seems, is to walk among us in the image of God, our Maker, whom we know not. (I feel much of that screaming crowd's anger was sheer frustration that this Man seemed to know it all – yet that very All lay beyond their grasp.)

'You will know that I do nothing of myself . . . I do always what pleases him.'

This saying tries to offer us – born upon fragile human words – the true nature of God. That he walks among us in love, in service, in humility. And this Son of Man, now speaking in the ancient Temple, where priests have long claimed valid commerce with God, will be taken outside the walls of Jerusalem to be crucified, lifted up, as the single, final sacrifice.

Listen with heart: can this be the Truth? God's Son, Son of Man, is willing to be killed so that he may return to his Father as peacemaker between man and God. This is the plan, this is pleasing to God.

Resulting in this final gift, his Guide, 'the Spirit of my Truth': Love itself, with us all our ways. 'To whom the world never gives ear.'

my Spirit of Truth is yours all ways

When you have lifted up
the Son of Man
then you will know
that I am he

You will know
that I do nothing
of myself

Only what the Father
has given me
do I teach

He who sent me
is with me
He never leaves me
to myself

for I do always what pleases him

I shall ask the Father
and he will give you your Guide
he will be with you all your ways
he is the Spirit of my Truth
to whom the world never gives ear

based on John 8, 14

Christ is risen in us

Those turbulent last days, culmination of a week of mounting crisis: crucifixion, obliteration by the worst public death imaginable. Then the unbelievable: evidence of New Life, transforming all who witnessed it.

We still struggle to make sense of our Easter, year by year. It should all change, we say, just as it did for them. Yet life goes on ... as it did for them. For nothing *was* changed instantly. There were still unbelievers, and runaways; and the whole group of them lay low for days and weeks before anyone dared stir out. Save, I imagine, the women bringing in food and news from the city.

The symbols and imagery of Easter are many; plenty here to play with. The empty tomb echoes our empty hearts. Bread is spread upon the table: we are invited to eat, to drink – the Staff of Life, our support upon our way. That distant dawn still offers to lighten our darkness. I may still run away from the reality of Love on offer; then I find he steals up behind me and falls in step alongside: Emmaus re-enacted.

My journey is never over. And I need all the help I may get. The secret is to remain open, to allow this persistent Easter energy continually to return me to Life, not just living.

Repeating susurrations of waves breaking upon the shore, my Maker, my Keeper, my Lover are persistent in their invitation.

Prayer is Love: Love itself new Life.

Christ is risen in us

Your emptying
fills us

Again-Maker
touch us today

Our Bread is baked
to succour us

Fountain
quench our thirst

Light
expel our darkness

Fall into step with us
along our Way

Teacher of Truth
mend our muddled mind

Vine planted in our midst
we drink your wine of Love

Life risen
lift us into your Death
to share your Love

Maker
Keeper
Lover

JOHN SKINNER
Easter 2006

they are become children of God

Cyprian, who was martyred in AD 258, was a great devotee of the writings of Tertullian who had taught in Carthage in the previous generation. His own writings – when he was not refereeing rebellious heretics – were less extensive but have a sincere hallmark of a prayerful man. His commentary on the Lord's Prayer is one of the earliest of the Fathers and still reads fresh today.

Echoing John's Gospel prelude, Cyprian addresses our new calling as children of God. 'You must be born again,' Jesus tells a baffled Nicodemus, the Jewish worthy, who came to him under cover of darkness. For all his learning, he honours Jesus as teacher, Rabbi, 'For no one could perform the signs you do unless God were with him.'

Nicodemus takes this born-again invitation too literally. But Jesus is speaking images that spell his alarming invitation.

'Unless a man is born through water and the Spirit, he cannot enter the Kingdom of God's family: what is born of flesh, remains flesh; who is born of the Spirit is spirit.' But still his questing visitor is silent. Jesus tries once more.

'You must be born from above. Take the wind, it blows wherever it will; you cannot see where it comes from or where it is bound. That is how it is with all who are born of the Spirit.'

John's Gospel begins with the Baptist recognizing Jesus as 'the Chosen One of God'. And the very next day, Jesus begins to call his friends, invite them to his side. 'Rabbi,' they ask, 'where do you live?' 'Come and see.'

In our prayer, Cyprian tells us, we encounter the Word who offers the very same invitation issued to his disciples, to Nicodemus. Prayer, this silent prayer now, is encounter. We are called by name, our own name, first uttered over the waters of baptism. 'Come and see ...' 'He gave them power to become Children of God ...' Our Easter invitation ...

they are become children of God

Our Father
who art in heaven

Mankind is made anew
born again
reconciled to his God
by grace

So our prayer begins
with his Word
who calls us
to be children of his Father

He came to his own domain
but his own people did not accept him

But to all who did receive him
he gave them his Power
to become Children of God

SAINT CYPRIAN
on the Lord's Prayer

MAY

MAY

our meal of Love

Christ's Easter enactment is revealed in the Eucharist. Here is the whole story, retold, lived again, his grace and power and love shared with all who come to this unique meal.

The danger is that the Mystery escapes us because we become so familiar with the repeating formula. Like the *Our Father* which I utter over and over, smothering its vital meaning: this is the Son of Man trusting me with his own words to his Father. The Word came into our world, and we make him mundane.

There exist many different renderings of the Lord's Prayer across the centuries. And it is a good exercise to compose one's own personal version, loosening up the words, breaking out their meaning. And I have attempted a similar task in composing my own narrative of the Eucharist.

Like fast food from a motorway stop-over, we can become inured to the deep Mystery of our meal. So let me ponder now its hidden meaning, the reality wrapped in this humble symbolism: a shared meal, an invitation that will satisfy my deepest need, Divine commerce bringing unwonted intimacy.

The Last Supper, which seemed at the time a final farewell, has become the paschal meal echoing down the ages, inviting all who will listen and attend to share and participate in the Mystery of the Father's gift of his Son, seated at the head of our table. The Son of Man gathers in his human family ...

our meal of Love

The Mystery of this meal
we will never understand
we simply live it
now
with You

First your invitation
Why us
Because you know our hunger
so we come to this your table
empty handed

Now
we take and break
this Bread
your Gift
of your Living Self
We share it among ourselves
Wait to give it to others in need

You feed the multitude
yet you know each person's special need

We take this cup
We are ever thirsty in this desert
You meet our thirst
with this red loving cup
We thank you Father
as we pass it among ourselves
drinking in all your many gifts
especially the Presence of your Living Love
Body of Christ
make me whole
Blood of Christ
make me giddy with your Love

JOHN SKINNER

Love's paradox

John of the Cross played with paradox all his life. It seemed to him that the nearer God came to him, the further he seemed apart.

The paradox of the saints is that while they should be our friends and close guide, we put them on a pedestal, so high as to become unreachable. And we behave similarly towards God himself. Somehow we know innately that he is beyond our grasp: the God of silence, the Invisible, the hidden One.

After a while, a kind of truce sets in: leave me alone and I'll pay you lip service.

John was much more hands on. While he grieved for his absent God, he knew the reason why.

> Where have you hidden
> Leaving me bereft, my Love?
> You sped away like a deer
> But first you had pierced me through
> I called aloud after you
> and tried to follow
> Now you are nowhere to be found
>
> John of the Cross, *Spiritual Canticle*

'John of the Cross speaks to people who feel unable to change. We may have sensed in our lives a call to freedom, to wholeness, to more than what we are now. John felt this as a call to reach out for God. But within us, an unvoiced fear can make change impossible. It is the fear that when we reach, we may not find. It begs the question: If I give myself, will God fill me in my life?'

So speaks Iain Matthew in *The Impact of God*, his gem that distils the spirit of John. 'John has taken the risk of surrender ... he is one who has been there. He testifies to a God who, precisely, is pressing in to meet, to change, and to fill us in our deepest need.

Love's paradox

God is always ready

but
we are very unready

God is so near to us

but
we are far from Him

God is within

but
we stray without

God is our home

but
we are still strangers
to his Love

JOHN OF THE CROSS

Truth sees God

Truth, wisdom, love: once again, Julian sews her words deftly, each separate stitch exactly in place, her overall design brightly coloured, drawing us into her meaning.

And what is her meaning? For myself, I feel she is showing how prayer is intimately linked to God's own inner reality which spills out into his created world: in Truth, in Wisdom and in embracing Love.

The human soul cannot bear very much reality. So we must rely upon God's generous gift. Our prayer is his doing, his active Love springing from deep within our home ground. We must seek his Truth, garner his Wisdom and from this diligence comes our harvest of Love.

The truth is that our Maker wishes us to know him. He already knows us, having fashioned us lovingly in every detail. But he stays with us, rocking our cradle as we awaken to all that it means to belong to his Divinely human family. In his wisdom, he has given his Son to be head of this family. He has laboured lifelong to provide for all; and his labours continue daily, nourishing our every need. And as I recognize his working, I know that I am enfolded in his Love.

And all is of his making ... The Unmade has contrived to share his sovereign riches with his new family, the creation of his choice – in time and space.

In time and in space: we are here in our making, attempting to comprehend the simplicity of his planned giving. Julian shows it to us bright and translucent on her tapestry page; my task is to join this working within the compass of my own existence.

And my task is enabled through my encounter in silent prayer:

It sees God
It beholds God
It loves God

46

Truth sees God

Truth sees God

Wisdom beholds God

and of these two comes the third
a holy marvellous delight in God
which is Love

For where Truth and Wisdom truly are
there too is Love
flowing from them Both

And all is of God's making

For he Is
the endless sovereign Truth
endless sovereign Wisdom
endless sovereign Love
Unmade

And the soul is a creature in God
that has the same properties though they be made

It sees God
it beholds God
it loves God

JULIAN OF NORWICH
Revelation of Divine Love, ch. 44

our Father's children

John, the disciple whom Jesus loved; the youngest of his friends who followed him with youthful enthusiasm during his brief ministry; John who stood beside Mary at the foot of the Cross and to whom she was entrusted for life as he hung dying.

Now John is writing as an old man. Like Mary, he has kept all these things in his heart. With the simplicity of age, he is able to sum up Christ's message. As Son of Man, Word sent from God, he has spoken in deeds and in his teachings all that may be said in human terms of his Father. Now it is John's turn to pass this wisdom on to his disciples.

'Think of the Love the Father has lavished upon us . . .'

I often marvel at the sheer size of the stage that has been set for us: the complexity of our world, the majestic outreach of the entire Universe, the miniscule detail of each atom, the beautiful logic of the periodic table, the miraculous structure of the human DNA helix, winged beauty as a swallow beats across the water meadow. But be not dazzled or bemused. Read this book of life as an intimation of his personal Love: 'I see his blood upon the rose and in the stars the glory of his eyes' (Joseph Mary Plunkett).

John takes our Divine adoption seriously: 'He calls us his children.'

Now imagine you have never known your own father, only heard tell of him. Wouldn't you yearn to meet him, see him with your very own eyes, be held at last in his arms.

Children, his children, that is who we are. John assures us. And then he offers sure proof: as children of our Father 'we shall see him as he really is'. Our birth certificate – 'children of God' – is verified by this future promise of unimaginable intimacy, to see God, 'my Father and your Father'.

'We shall be like him.'

our Father's children

Think
of the Love
the Father has lavished upon us

He calls us his children

That is who we are
because we shall see him
as he really is

The world ignores him
and so
the world ignores us

We are already his children
but what we are to be
has not been revealed

All we know now
is that when it is revealed
we shall be like him

based on 1 John 3

JUNE

JUNE

our faith is our light

As with Julian, so with prayer: the Three are in active, dynamic relationship – within and without. For as Julian treats of God, without fail she names the Trinity; not as some numerical conundrum but as an experienced relationship, communicating itself to her in person. 'I had in part, touching, sight and feeling in three properties of God.'

I deliberately introduced Julian's mantra, 'I it am', early as one of the January readings: it is a key to her meaning and a vital message to us about prayer. I pointed out the link back to Moses: God appeared as mysterious fire hovering over a thorn bush in the desert. Moses knew his Maker but was bold enough to ask his name: 'I am who I am', he was told.

For Moses, God, the future lawgiver and protector of his people, was the One God. Through Jesus we have learned more about the dynamic community that is God's inner and outward 'Am-ness': Life, Love and Light. Julian tells us how she was touched – in her praying, as we also may be touched – by 'marvellous homeliness, gentle courtesy, endless nature'.

Each time we pray, entering our silent inner world, we invite Jesus himself to break our silence with his own prayer of love and recognition of his Father. The Father smiles at this exchange: his smile, the kiss of Love.

'I had in part, touching . . .' Only in part, that is all we ask for: the rest is 'in our night, which light is God, our endless day'.

our faith is our light

I had in part touching sight and feeling
in three properties of God
where many times it was said
'I it am'

Life Love and Light

In Life is marvellous homeliness
in Love there is gentle courtesy
in Light there is endless nature

These three properties
were in one Goodness

Our faith is a light
kindly coming from our endless day
that is our Father, God

In which light
our Mother Christ
and our good Lord the Holy Spirit
lead us in this passing life

Thus I saw and understood
that our faith is our light
in our night
which light is God
our endless day

JULIAN OF NORWICH
Relevation of Divine Love, ch. 83

drunk with joy

I am often teased by my friends (and I don't tease easy) for being garrulous about silence. What is to be said about this Carthusian poet who sings aloud so sweetly in his cell?

The first is that he wishes to remain anonymous. And second, that he minds not one wit if I publish his poem – 'if it might be of any help to people ...'

'I walk primeval waters and have no fear: the Miracle of Living, it leaves me stunned.' I think many people would be stunned to learn that a man who appears so poor that he has given up everything, can sing with such open delight at the joys of his existence. What are we outsiders missing?

'Blessed are the poor in spirit ... the Kingdom is already theirs.'

'This day you will be with me in Paradise . . . the Kingdom is among you.'

These are the two clues. Poverty of spirit is not simply poverty, having nothing. Poverty of spirit is awakening to my utter dependence upon my Maker, making real that relationship. I like to think that my Carthusian friends do nothing, they simply take God for real. And that takes a lifetime.

No, we can't all dash off to the cloister: that is to miss the point. But, *pace* Professor Dawkins, God is no delusion – he takes me for real and I must reciprocate. How? Our poet spells it out: accept 'the Miracle of Living'.

The heart-rending moment of faith on Calvary, when the Dying Thief turns to Jesus and calls him a just man, is our perfect prayer. For it sums up our poverty of spirit: Dismas had nothing left, he was at death's door; indeed, his very name is Greek for 'dying'. And here is the Son of Man dying with him, so his prayer makes him the richest man on earth. He sees the Kingdom and accepts it with open arms.

I too am dying: I plead each moment that I may have Life. That is the Miracle of Living, to have not and yet to have all.

drunk with joy

I walk primeval waters and have no fear
The Miracle of Living
it leaves me stunned
Day and night I walk in a daze
This power to be
to breathe to live
this power to think
to hope to love
and the cost
The air is free
the heavens are free
Jesus remember me
This day you will be with me in Paradise

I walk chaotic depths and have no fear
The miracle of grace
to be free of sin
by Christ's death
free of the burden of guilt
is life freshly given
a new surge of hope
of fearlessness in the face of death
The abysmal sea
Jesus remember me
This day you will be with me in Paradise

I walk the tumultuous main and have no fear
the miracle of trust
Goodness devoid of boundaries
inspires trust devoid of doubt
I'm stone drunk with joy
at the thought of God
My heart runs to meet him
my feet skim the sea
Jesus remember me
This day you will be with me in Paradise

A CARTHUSIAN

55

waiting room

Marie-Claire tells me that she wrote this spare and beautiful poem as an exercise on a poetry-writing course. The invitation was to write a poem about waiting. And in a moment of inspiration, she thought of waiting upon God in her prayer.

People's first reaction to silent prayer is 'What am I to do with all my noise and distractions?' Our poet has an answer 'carve a calm space' and let all that float by. The image of a fisherman comes to mind. He sits on the river bank with his rod, gently eyeing his float. That is the key to his waiting. When that bobs under, he knows he is in business. All else simply floats past his gaze to be lost downstream.

When we come regularly to our inner sanctum, silence and peace soon well up. And this is not of our doing: we may not make prayer, for true prayer is a gift. All we may do is the waiting . . . for the Three are already present. For this inner sanctum is of their making.

waiting room

A hiatus of calm. Space

carved out of clutter.

Time suspended.

Fistfuls of minutes shredded,

second by slow second.

An inner room, a sanctum

of peace. A hiatus of calm

space. Of waiting.

Waiting.

MARIE-CLAIRE KAMINSKI

our three powers

Meister Eckhart never ceases to thrill me: his certainty allied to his bold originality. Here he reaches back to Augustine's *De Trinitate*, picking up on the three powers or functions of the mind's Soul – memory, understanding and my will. But whereas Augustine spreads himself to over four hundred pages, our preacher confines himself to a simple Sunday sermon offered to the people of Cologne. I sometimes wonder what they thought as they filed out of church into the square – stunned silence or a buzz of discussion.

'Mind, will and rage – our life-giving relationship with the Trinity.'

An artist creating something unique can be said to have put himself into his work. God puts his own image into all that he has made: the whole of creation echoes back to manifest its source. 'My Father loves me from eternity': he utters the Word, his Wisdom, by which he knows and loves, a love which is reciprocated. Supremely, it is mankind who echoes the image of our Maker. There was an inevitability that the Word would become the Son of Man; for in God there is no half measure – this was the only way he would communicate his Love for the human family whom he is fashioning.

Yes, present tense: his working is now, within us all. Deep within the human soul our Maker is working the image of himself.

Mind: 'Keep my word in your heart and so live in my Love.'

Will: giver of Life, gift of fecundity – your Will be mine.

Rage: rage at myself for fearing to receive the gift of Life.

Come aside and pray with me awhile ...

our three powers

The soul has been given three powers
mind
will
and rage

These three powers are our life-giving relationship
with the Trinity

'Love each other
as I have always loved you
My Father loves me from Eternity
so do I love you
Keep my Word in your heart
and so live in my Love'

Will cleaving to the Father can do all things
'I do always the will of my Father'

The Father
source of all
pours into the human soul
creative power
unique fecundity

Mind cleaving to the Son
knows with the Son
it knows with the Son
when it is void of knowledge

The third power is the power of attack
the Living birth of the Spirit

MEISTER ECKHART
Sermo xviii

JULY

JULY

God's Silence

In this masterly passage, Henri Nouwen leads us into the mind of John whose opening passage of his Gospel recapitulates the creation story announced in Genesis revealing how creation is now fulfilled in the person of Christ.

Through the Word God has uttered all creation: in the Word he re-creates and makes it whole again. Both creation itself and Christ's task of refashioning it is an ongoing process. Creation is not a seven-day wonder which happened long ago; creation is happening now, under our very feet, before our eyes. Even age-old rock and stone is held in being by the active will of our Maker. Each spring is a new creation, a fresh beginning. So too each human birth announces a new start as the process of life opens to its limitless potential. Limitless because the human journey of change and growth has no finite end: our goal is God himself, alpha and omega, my beginning, my end.

And the Word is my companion in this 'way of the heart', as Nouwen names it. 'He gives power to all who believe in him to become children of God.' Yet this awesome journey is wrapped in mist, for it is a way of faith. The Word of God has been spoken deep in the silence of the human heart; it is here that 'He unfolds the immeasurable richness of his Silence.'

God's Silence

Out of eternal silence
God spoke the Word
Through his Word
he creates and recreates
the world

In the beginning
God spoke
land sea and sky
God spoke the sun moon the stars
God spoke
plants birds fish animals wild and tame

Finally
God spoke
man and woman

Then in the fullness of time
God's Word
through whom all had been created
became Flesh
and gave power
to all who believe
to become
children of God

In all this
the Word of God
does not break the Silence of God
He unfolds
the immeasurable richness
of his Silence

HENRI NOUWEN
The Way of the Heart

the prayer is always within

Prayer is never something I do. It precedes any human activity; for prayer is a relationship with our Source, the One from whom we come, to whom we go. In this sense, alone, 'prayer is always within'. But we must go further.

Our Source, the unfathomable Trinity, may be likened to an eternal model of immeasurable Love – a dynamic pulsar beyond our time and space. Words, leaf-like human words that fail in all respects. Eckhart tells us that we can never say anything about God without denying at once what we say. But we can know God through his Word: Christ in his deeds, in his words, above all in his Person. For it is this same Jesus, the Risen Christ, who comes to me in my silent prayer.

It is all a question of listening. Being and receiving: not doing. No human words or deeds are needed in this relationship. We have Christ himself as our prayer. And this is the prayer who is always within. He echoes my faint strivings of love and seeking, gathering them in his own Self-Giving of Love for the Father – in the Spirit of prayer, the Spirit of Love, always within.

the prayer is always within

Remember said my friend
prayer is always within

Not like a television
noising to an empty room
Even sadder emptier still

Your silent conversation
your reaching out to me
your giving love
is always mine
for the listening

Yet I do not hear
fail to listen

Your silent attention
is my very life
given each moment
Your talk is never small talk
but the cavernous silence of your eternal love

Teach me to listen
to my prayer
that you gave to me
long ago
are giving
Now

Son of Man
murmuring the Love
of our Father
always within

JOHN SKINNER

psalm of courage

This modern psalm, partly paraphrasing Isaiah 41, was sent to me by a friend. It comes from a huge body of similar psalm prayers written over a period of years by John Hammersley. In all, John wrote 150 psalms before he died in November 2004; they may be accessed on his website for private and public use and may be freely distributed with attribution.

The human condition is essentially lonely. I seem to come into this wide world alone and I will leave it as this individual dies. Isaiah sees things differently.

> Listen, Jacob my servant, Israel whom I have chosen,
> Yahweh, your Maker, speaks.
> I formed you from the womb and am your help:
> Do not be afraid for it is I who have chosen you.

The Chosen People continually turned to false gods, so that Isaiah must cajole, threaten then woo them back to an open relationship with Yahweh. It can be summed up simply as taking God at his Word.

We all make false gods, cunningly chosen to distance ourselves from the One who alone can close in on our aloneness. Make no mistake: God is not about to live my life for me. The deal is that he 'comes in quietness ... moves me on gently'. Once that is understood, then I may be open to my many human relationships which flow from and express God's living love for me.

All this takes courage. Yet keep it simple and it comes alive.

psalm of courage

Do not be frightened or worried
for I am your God and I am always with you

Be determined and confident
Since you are mine
I will always support you

I am the God of love who moves you gently on
leading you drawing you into all that is new and lovely

All you need is available now
Let me carry you and bear you along in safety

I am the Lord of Love who comes to you in quietness
There's no need to struggle or panic

I died for you in the cruelty of torture
how can I let you suffer alone

I am the Spirit of Love to direct you tenderly
I hold your hand and will not hurry you

We will go together into tomorrow
For I am with you and I won't let you go

Be not afraid for I am with you
I shall never abandon you wherever you may fall

Only be strong and very courageous
For you are mine and I will always love you

JOHN HAMMERSLEY
www.psalmsoflife.com

sound deep

George Fox, founder of the Quakers, was a man of single mind who travelled thousands of miles to preach and teach his vision of Christ's message.

The start of his movement happened when he climbed Pendle Hill, high above the Ribble Valley in Lancashire. 'I went to the top of it with much ado, it was so steep; but I was moved by the Lord to go atop of it.' When he regained his breath, he preached for three hours to a gathering of about a thousand.

From Seekers they became Finders, came the report.

Fox thought that organized religion had grown too complicated. He never set foot in a church, dubbing them steeple houses and imploring their priest-masters to repent!

What he said upon his Lancashire mountain top was never recorded but a phrase echoes down to us from his hill: 'Keep your feet upon the top of the mountain and sound deep to that of God in everyone.'

Three hours condensed to a single bidding: after that Silence among Friends. Certainly, we conceive of today's Quakers as peaceful men and admire the economy of their faith. But at root silence is a powerful, sometimes threatening experience. As Elijah found when he was asked by God, 'What are you doing here?'

We read in 1 Kings 19 that he was then told, 'Go and stand before Yahweh': Then Yahweh himself went by. Then came a great wind, so strong it tore into the mountain and shattered rocks. But Yahweh was not in that wind. After the wind, a fire. But Yahweh was not in the fire. And after the fire – the whisper of the faintest breeze.

We mistake God for an earthquake if we think we may conjure him in our prayer. The simplicity of silence is that it cuts me out of the action, so that if I listen, I may just catch that faintest whisper of his breeze.

'Sound deep' to his presence in everyone is to say the same. For he is not in the earthquake, the fire, the wind, but everywhere and in everyone.

'I am who I am.'

sound deep

Mountains
are tough to climb
as is life
but the view from the top
is awesome

Mountain tops
are for praying
staying
where we find ourselves
in peace

Deep inside
ourselves
within us all
if we listen
we will hear
his Word

'Keep your feet upon the top
of the mountain

and sound deep
to that of God
in everyone'

GEORGE FOX
preaching to the Seekers

69

AUGUST

AUGUST

infinite space

Rector of Credenhill, near Hereford, for his entire priestly ministry, Thomas Traherne left us a record of his spiritual journey both in his extensive poetry and an ambitious journal *Centuries of Meditations*. In many ways, he reminds me of Hopkins: we only begin to know and love the man long after he is dead. Not that Traherne was entirely ignored in his lifetime; Sir Orlando Bridgeman, Keeper of the Seals to Charles II, appointed him his private chaplain. But even this lofty appointment seems not to have turned his head or purpose. For he continued to spend most of his time and energies in his country parish.

This brief but burning passage well illustrates the metal of the man. It often astonishes me how great minds think alike. In this single passage, Traherne, who is clearly speaking from an intense distillation of his own inner experience, repeats almost word for word similar sayings of Meister Eckhart and Julian of Norwich.

The human soul, Julian is speaking, is not merely created by its Maker, we are continually sustained by our Keeper:

> See I am God.
> See I am in all thing.
> See I do all thing.
> See I never lift my hands off my own works,
> nor ever shall, without end. How should anything be amiss?

And again Julian assures us:

> God is nearer to us than our own soul;
> for he is the ground in whom our soul stands.
> Our soul sits in God in very rest
> and our soul stands in God for very strength
> and our soul is kindly rooted in God in endless love.

infinite space

Infinity we know
and feel by our Souls

Feel it so naturally
as the very Essence
and Being of the Soul

The truth is
it is individually in the Soul
for God is there

more near to us
than we are to our Selves

So that we cannot feel our Souls
but we must feel Him

in that first of Properties
Infinite Space

THOMAS TRAHERNE (1637–1674)
Poet-Priest

73

the Father's plan

Richard Dawkins tells us we are deluded by God. That is because Richard Dawkins, being a tidy scientist, likes to put everything in its place. So that when it comes to God, he finds himself empty handed. The only ploy left to him is to blame gullible believers for embarrassing him in the first place. Why can't we see things his way and give God a wide berth. Leave him alone, out in the cold.

The problem is, dear Doctor Dawkins, God won't let *me* alone. But you are right: he has his problems. The main problem is one of levels of existence. It is rather annoying to the tidy, if circumscribed, scientific mind, to conceive of a Being who is inconceivable. Sorry, but that's the way it is. Moreover, this Infinite Being seems to be mostly about Love. That is to say, he doesn't stay at home and hug himself for all his perfect Infinity and Impenetrability. He decides to go outside himself and share his riches with the finite world which he has made.

No Richard, not in seven days flat, you can have that one. But scientists certainly didn't make the world: their sole task is to fathom its endlessly beautiful design.

Now let's listen to John. John who lived with Christ, got to know him, heard his words, witnessed his actions. And when he was finally gone, John summed up his life in a word – love. His love he had left behind. Greater than human love, it filled the lives of his friends, informing and changing them.

They had not seen God, but they had seen and touched and lived with Christ who called himself the Son of Man, the Word spoken by the invisible Father. 'As we love each other, so God lives in us: his Love finds its fulfilment in us.'

A simple plan. God likes to keep it simple. It is we humans who tend to complicate, especially dead cert. religious as well as dead cert. scientists: we are all at it together. Let the woman at the well bring us to our senses. It was she who boasted to all and sundry in her village: 'He has told me all about myself.'

the Father's plan

No one
has ever seen God
but as we love each other
God lives in us
and his love
finds fulfilment in us

We know now
that we are living in God
and he lives in us
for he has poured
his Spirit
upon us
his Spirit of our Love

The time has come

True worshippers
will find the Father
in Spirit
and in Truth

This is the Father's invitation
the Father's plan
for his human family

based on 1 John 4; John 4:23

most is least

Meister Eckhart, the great German mystic and teacher, saw God's dealings, the Father's plan, as a paradox. The relationship between Maker and his creatures can present itself to them in no other guise. So we must go along with it, with our human eyes closed but our inner eyes, the eyes of faith, wide open to his light.

It becomes a question of trust and faith. 'Does a father give a stone rather than a warm loaf of bread?'

'The Word was made Flesh to dwell among us.' And he continues to dwell among us in our daily lives. But this is no takeover; we are not to hand the reins of our lives over to another, all problems solved. My life is *my* life to live and own up to. He walks alongside as equal partner in exploring the depths and fullest meaning of my human existence. I must be ever more sensitive to his presence, the gentlest of hints, the gift of his constancy and love.

'I am the light shining in your darkness ... walk with me.'

No visions, no voices, no blinding lights – but a steady process, a journey in love and understanding of what it is to live as a human being – just like him, the Word among us still.

most is least

Frequently a thing small to us
God sees as large
So we should take all he sends blindly
taking his lead
in our feelings
in what happens
For he gives us most in his least
without fail

The Word
was made Flesh
to dwell among us

He understands
underpins
walks with us
in this our mundane life

His lives as we live alongside
caring
counting each small footstep

Attend
watch with me
walk as I walked
am walking
with you

I am the Light
shining in your darkness
Close your eyes
your ears
to the world
and walk with Me
Where to us God shows least he is often most

MEISTER ECKHART
Last Words

77

Silence – the profound activity of listening love

A Carthusian describes his day, a routine of rhythm and of Silence which encapsulates his entire life. From the moment he awakens, this hermit-poet monk turns his attention to the silent beauty of his Maker. It is still morning but all around the cloister, each in his separate cell-house, the community of silent monks wash, dress and begin their day. Prime is recited, then silent prayer until the bell summons the white-clad monks, cowls covering their bowed heads, to church for their morning Eucharist.

'Silent on the way to duty: silent on the way to Silence, where the Word unspoken dwells.'

And their day stretches out ahead, one day following another. Until each individual is invited to enter his final door:

'Silent on the way to Silence, where the longed-for Jesus dwells.'

It is a mysterious calling to a way of life which often baffles, irritates or even angers, the outsider. But I believe the Carthusian message of silence to the world at large is a wonderful gift, a gentle, whispered invitation.

'Do you know about Silence, John?' I was asked by the Prior when first I went to stay at Parkminster. 'Yes,' I replied, knowing that I would have to respect the silence that was tangible and inviting throughout the monastery. I had yet to appreciate its true depth and power.

Even in our busy lives today, there are times of silence. We may welcome them, use the silence or discard it as empty and a waste of time. In that, we would be wrong. For silence is the deep well within, the frontier where we wait, 'in the face of beauty, in the morning light; where the Word unspoken dwells'.

Silence is given to us all; ours to guard, to nurture and to grow in.

Yes, I am beginning to understand silence, more and more ...

Silence – the profound activity of listening love

Silent
in the face of beauty

Silent
in the morning light

Silent
on the way of duty

Silent
in the awesome Light

Silent
on the way to Silence
where the Word
unspoken dwells

Silent
on the way to Silence
where
the longed-for Jesus
dwells

A CARTHUSIAN

SEPTEMBER

SEPTEMBER

autumn 2003

Let us stay with our gifted Carthusian poet. He has much to say to us; he speaks through his Silence. For his silent ways have sharpened his senses; he sees and feels the reality behind everyday things. His silence permits him to conjure words most skilfully; then share his vision with me.

Parkminster nestles beneath the Sussex Downs. And each Monday, a straggling file emerge from the great doors of St Hugh's Charterhouse. They are dressed in their white habits, they clomp two by two in their walking boots. Here come the monks: dogs bark but bystanders greet them warmly. It is as if they know they are somehow blessed by this brief passing.

Two by two. Then the companies change, so that over the day each monk walks with a different companion. Their conversation pleasant, never urgent, gentle, never strained; and as they pass through fields, over stiles, along the riverbank, a heron rises, floating above their heads. There is time aplenty for our poet to drink in the scene.

He sees these autumn colours like banners carried into battle. Conflict here: the turning of the year. Summer slowly retreats as winter chill advances victorious. But all is meant to be. This dying has its purpose. We have seen it many times before.

'Unless the grain falls into the earth and dies . . . I must be lifted up, then all shall know me.'

This white phalanx wending its way up across the Downs is like the fiery multitudinous leaves; their silence shouts across Sussex and beyond. These are the silent martyrs trumpeting the beauty of God's love for all his human family. As they pass, their shadow falls upon me and I murmur my silent thanks to have known them all too briefly. But know them just the same.

autumn 2003

Autumn slipped in unawares; the sun

So bright deceived me. I felt the summer stay

Lingering in warm fields and bridle paths.

But there was revolution on every side:

The multitudinous leaves, a sunset host,

Turned yellow in little lanes, hung like fire

On peach and pear; all were up in arms,

Had overgrown summer and cast their fruit

To mother earth. They knew from the deep say,

From the nip in the wind; they knew and made a last

Shout across Sussex, a fanfare of beauty

Dying like holy martyrs in the blood of duty . . .

A Carthusian

how should anything be amiss?

The story Julian tells of how she received sixteen showings or communications as she lay at death's door is remarkable enough. Yet their actual content are uniquely arresting. All bear a similar message: that God is immanent and always actively present in all creation, especially to each human individual he has lovingly generated. Yet each showing finds a distinct voice. Julian herself spent over twenty years meditating and digesting 'his meaning'. Finally, she sums up quite simply: 'love was his meaning'.

Her own prayer was often heavy going. 'Many times our trust is not complete; we are not sure whether God hears us, or so it seems, owing to our unworthiness, and we feel quite empty.' Does that ring familiar? And then she is answered:

> I am the ground of your beseeking: first it is my will that you have it, and then I make you want it: now since I make you seek, and then you do seek, how should it then be that you should not have *whom* you seek?

See how prayer is not about asking, endless shopping lists, but about our relationship with our Maker. And it is he who initiates the substance of our prayer: he who is present all the while.

'See I am God. See I am in all thing. See I do all thing ...'

Whoever described an absent God? Here, quite literally, we have a 'hands on' God: 'see I never lift my hands off my own works ...'

And it is Julian's signature in all her writing that she sees God's activity as the Trinity at work within the ground of the human soul.

'I lead all thing ... with the same Might, Wisdom, Love that I made it: how should anything be amiss?'

how should anything be amiss?

See I am God

See I am in all thing

See I never lift my hands off my own works
nor ever shall
without end

See I lead all thing
to the end I ordained for it
from without beginning

with the same
Might
Wisdom
and Love
that I made it

How should anything be amiss?

JULIAN OF NORWICH
The Third Showing

'I can tell you Dr Manning, that I 'ad me bishop's mitre on me 'ead when you were still an 'eretic!' Such was the rebuke awarded to Cardinal Manning when he sought to criticize the close friendship between John Henry Newman of the nearby Oratory and the long-serving Bishop of Birmingham.

William Bernard Ullathorne was a man to be reckoned with. He left school at twelve to join his father's business; but at the age of fifteen he went to sea for four years. Rather like Saint Patrick at a similar age, the young cabin boy was touched by prayer: he attended Mass in a Baltic port and his life changed. He came home and presented himself as a novice to the Benedictines at Downside. Ordained priest in 1833, he volunteered for missionary work and left for New South Wales to become vicar general. At the time, there were just three other priests in the entire colony, it being administered from Mauritius. After eight years of pioneering work, Australia's first bishop arrived, accompanied by a group of priests; Ullathorne was then free to return home. When, in 1850, the Roman Catholic Hierarchy was restored, not without public controversy, he was appointed the first Bishop of Birmingham, a position he was to hold for the next thirty-eight years.

Rough diamond he may have been, but Ullathorne speaks with direct experience about his approach to prayer. I find it remarkable that a man who had travelled thousands of miles at sea, both as boy and priest, should state so brilliantly that we must find God within ourselves: 'God is everywhere, but not everywhere for us.' The one single point in the whole of God's expansive universe where we may be met – 'where God connects with us ... is in the centre of our own soul ...' This is where we encounter 'our true Self' as we own up to the true nature of our being.

Meister Eckhart endorses this simple truth with a devastating statement which invites me to prolonged silence.

interior encounter

Let this be understood
we cannot turn to God
unless we first
enter into ourselves

God is everywhere
but not everywhere for us

There is one point in the universe
where God connects with us

that is the centre of our own soul
our true Self

There he waits for us
there he meets us

To see him we enter our own interior

BISHOP ULLATHORNE (1806–1889)

We meet
in the Ground of the Soul
the True Image of God in man

MEISTER ECKHART

be-coming

The Ladder of Monks was written in the twelfth century by Guigo II who was, in succession to Saint Bruno, the ninth Prior of La Grande Chartreuse. He is somewhat quaintly known as Guigo II since a first Guigo had preceded him as fifth prior. He had enormous influence within the Order for it was under his guidance that the first Statutes were written detailing the oral Carthusian traditions left them by Bruno, their founder.

Guigo II, however, was to influence the world outside with his modest letter to a fellow Carthusian informing him of an insight he had had about prayer. So influential was this intriguing document that it was rapidly copied and spread in all directions. As time passed, its true authorship became buried – such is the anonymity of Carthusian writers – and it began to be attributed first to Augustine and then to Bernard.

The key to the letter's importance is that it sets out to analyse the steps by which a monk may advance in prayer; and notably it proclaims, for the first time, the importance of *lectio divina*.

Guigo writes to his friend and fellow Carthusian, 'Brother Gervase', offering him four steps: reading, meditation, prayer and contemplation. These steps, he suggests, are like Jacob's ladder reaching up to heaven. So that now a simple monk may also use this ladder ...

Barely four centuries ago, it was inconceivable that everyone might have access to the Word of God in their own tongue. Only recently did we leave the matter of praying to the professionals behind convent and monastery walls. Today, prayer is a free-for-all, and very many take their daily prayer for real.

All the more reason to seek good guidance; and Guigo is on hand with his simple ladder. I read a sacred text, slowly and with interior recollection. Here, Guigo uses the metaphor of chewing our food, tasting it well before it is digested. We may mull these insights and meditate upon them, before petitioning God in prayer for all our needs. Then comes his response, the gift of his Love which we may receive at any time of his discretion. All is gift: but first I must prepare the table for my meal.

be-coming

Praying is my be-coming
my coming alive to my being
in the Presence
of my Maker

I read your Word
digesting slowly
tasting your meaning

I pray to understand more
who I am
in your Presence

Father
through
and in
your Word
you breath me forth

I receive your breath of Life
and breathe Love
back
to You

JOHN SKINNER
based on Guigo II,
The Ladder of Monks

OCTOBER

OCTOBER

at one

Plotinus sought to refine the philosophy of Plato; and in doing so, he had lasting influence on Jewish, Christian, Muslim as well as pagan philosophers and mystics. His chief work, *The Enneads*, was put together over his last seventeen years. They are drawn directly from lecture notes prepared for his pupils. But he shrank from the huge labour of putting them into good shape: finally, he handed the task to a trusted friend and former pupil.

Nowhere in this extensive work does he once refer to Christianity. So that to my mind, he demonstrates how all men are open to Divine inspiration. His last words were: 'Always try to give back the Divine in you to the Divine in the All.'

In his opening sentence in this brief passage – 'I often re-awaken ...' – Plotinus seems to offer a wonderful description of prayer. I like to see prayer as 'birthing', being made aware yet again of the gratuitous gift that is my Self. Deepening my hold on the source of Life, being touched within by my Maker.

'My She Self is open . . .' I well remember George Walkerley, my Jesuit novice master, saying 'all humankind are feminine in relating to God'; we may only receive and reflect back all that is given – Life, Love and all the rest. 'O Bonitas, now I see.'

When I pray, I am sometimes aware of all who pray with me ... now ... at this moment. And those who are asleep or unaware of the beauty of this possibility; and so I pray also with them. I pray too with all who have ever prayed; all those, like us, who had to strive to make this misty, mystical journey of faith. For them now this prayer is their reality, 'They see God face to face.'

Above all, I do not pray: for Christ prays within, without and for all:
'Father, into your eternal hands I pour my Spirit.'
'Always try to give back the Divine in you
to the Divine in the All.'

at one

Often I re-awaken
I move out of my body
to rest
within my Self

I come to be
outside other things
I am
inside my Self

O Bonitas
now
I see

My She Self
is open
is alert
for She
is Be Coming

I am Be Come
the Object
at one
with
One

PLOTINUS (205–270)
The Enneads

gazing at the light that never changes

Augustine of Hippo, born less than century after Plotinus, was another African nurtured within the learned culture of the Roman Empire. He too was untouched by Christianity until he travelled to Milan where he saw Ambrose, the bishop. The first thing that struck him was that this man was reading without moving his lips. Until then, Augustine, a rhetor whose job it was to speak, had always read aloud. He fell unwilling under the bishop's spell and later returned to Africa repenting his ungodly past to become the dominating influence in Christian thinking for the next 1000 years. Only then did other voices begin to be heard, dissenting from what had seemed certain orthodoxy.

So Augustine the thinker, pre-eminent theologian, tells us about a certain moment in prayer. How similar to Plotinus is his opening: he is guided to journey within, 'to the depths of my soul', and there he returns to his true self. Or as Plotinus of Alexandria describes his encounter 'the re-awakening'.

And see how Augustine, the great thinker, whose treatise on the Trinity runs to over 1000 pages, acknowledges that this experience is 'above my whole mind'. No thinking is needed as we pray: it is not of that order. I don't have to think as I meet my friend and familiar. Our relationship swings into life at once and we exchange hearts rather than minds. Lovers do not think or make plans; their love alone is their intent.

'With you as my guide ...' So too, in prayer – tuning into God's relationship with us – we need no human maps, no false techniques, even trusted methods will wear thin like a favourite pair of shoes. No, silent prayer is God's business: keep it simple, allow him to set the flow.

You might find Augustine's own flow somewhat overwhelming. He was a master of words: his Sunday sermons drew huge crowds into his church at Hippo. The phrase that sings to me is: 'all who know truth know this Light'. Remember John's prologue to his Gospel: 'The Word was the true light that enlightens all men ... to all who accepted him, he gave power to become children of God.'

Augustine towers above his peers just as Paul did when he burst upon the scene; both men knew how to set their signature upon their times and on into the future far ahead. Both were mystics, touched by God. But both would be the first to assure us that this touching, this intimate Loving presence, is for all. We must hold out our hands, hungry as we are:

'I am the food for all mankind. Grow and you shall eat me. I will change you into myself ...'

gazing at the light that never changes

With you as my guide I entered the depths of my soul
with you my only helper
I returned to my true self

With the eye of my soul
I saw far beyond
even above my whole mind
I was gazing at the Light that never changes

No ordinary light of day
nor just such a light far brighter
bright as the sun
This was no such light
but another far removed from all earthly light

And it shone above my mind
not as oil will float upon water
nor even as the heavens arch themselves above the earth
Simply – it was above my soul because it made me
I was below since I was made by it

All who know the Truth
know this Light at once for what it is
and all who see this Light know eternity
And love alone may see this Light

O Truth who is Eternity
Love who is Truth
Eternity who is Love
You are my God

I heard your voice calling me from high above:
'I am the food for all mankind
Grow and you shall eat me. I will change you into myself ...'
'I am who I am'

SAINT AUGUSTINE, (354–430)
Confessions, Bk 7:12

I it am

We met Julian's wonderful refrain at the head of the year as one of the January readings. I thought it so important to let her experience set the tone of Silent Prayer – the continuing encounter with the God who comes bringing his endless Love into my life.

Julian stayed silent in her cell huddled beside the little church of St Julian in Norwich for over twenty years. And during that time, she refined and came closer to her core experience which brought her here: that life-giving encounter with her dying Christ as she too – so all thought – lay near to death.

'I it am ...' Very Life itself: here, now, underpinning your every move, your thoughts, feelings, pulse beat. And it is in Silent Prayer that the dynamic presence of the Three begins to dawn as actual reality itself.

The Father's mighty goodness, source of all.
Our Mother Christ whispering the Wisdom of the Word
    spelling Truth.
The Light of the Spirit who is Love poured upon mankind.

My prayer becomes more real in as much as I allow the One and Three to touch me with their working:

'I am that makes you to love
I am that makes you to long
I it am ...'

I it am

I it am
the might
and the goodness
of the Fatherhood

I it am
the wisdom
of the Motherhood

I it am
the light
and the grace
that is all blessed Love

I
it
am
the Trinity

I it am
the Unity

I am
the sovereign Goodness
of all manner of things
I am that makes you to love
I am that makes you to long

I it am
the endless fulfilling
of all true desires

JULIAN OF NORWICH
Revelation of Divine Love, ch. 59

97

seeing the Father

The scene is familiar: the heady atmosphere of that last meal which John describes over five long chapters, mostly in Jesus' own words.

The question comes from Philip. He has heard so much about the Father on his Master's lips that he can contain himself no longer. 'Show him to us and then we will be satisfied at last ...' But Philip had misunderstood Christ's purpose, his meaning. Perhaps there is a sub-text here closer to home. John is coming to the end of his extraordinary story; he wants us to be quite clear. At the outset he has already named the Christ as Word of God. And Jesus had spelt it plain to Nicodemus, 'No one has gone up to heaven except the one who came down from heaven, the Son of Man who is in heaven.'

And even more explicitly, he teaches his mission in the synagogue at Capernaum: 'No one has seen the Father except the one who comes from God: he has seen the Father. Everyone who believes has eternal life. I am the Bread of Life, the living Bread which has come down from heaven. Anyone who eats this Bread will live forever.'

Strange words even for our ears today: no wonder Philip got in a muddle, taking things too literally.

So Jesus repeats his Word from the Father's lips as simply as he may: 'You will recognize that I am in my Father, and you in me and I in you ...'

In the Prayer of Silence may that recognition slowly dawn.

seeing the Father

Let us see the Father
then we shall be satisfied

To have seen me
is to have seen the Father
I am in the Father
and the Father is in me

You will recognize
that I am in my Father

and you in me

and I in you

based on JOHN 14

NOVEMBER

NOVEMBER

nada

People sometimes find my approach to prayer over optimistic. I make it sound so easy when in fact we all know praying is a continuous struggle. A friend once declared, 'I don't pray anymore, I did enough in the old days.' Another confessed, 'I stopped praying and then I left the Order ...' I suspect both were misled: the first because one can never finish praying, as one never stops breathing. And the second because he might have had a better time leaving if he had prayed through his crisis.

Prayer will ever remain a paradox: at once it is the most natural thing in the world, and it is other worldly. Think of the disciples, they saw Jesus pray and envied him. 'Show us how to pray,' they asked. Then when the true time of trial came, they first fell asleep and then took to their heels.

John of the Cross was eager to lead his Carmelite sisters into silent prayer. He was leaving them for a while and so fashioned a little card for each of them. Sixty or so ... some still exist. They show a crude sketch of a mountain and all the way up its slope runs a central path on which is repeated the word *nada, nada, nada*. Nothing. At the top a brief, enigmatic message 'There is no road here; because for the just there is no law – she is her own law.' As Christ promised us 'The Truth shall set you free.'

In other words, we must each find – or be shown – our own way up this twisting slope. There is certainly no easy way; but equally there is no one way. 'We don't really have a method ...' I was told by a Carthusian; I believe I heard him add under his breath, 'we just do it!'

And all the obvious common sense goes to the wall in this relationship. We must not be greedy but learn to taste nothing. We do not need equipment for this climb, the least the better. We need to discover our real Self and walk away from the person we think we would like to be. It is not about knowing, but about unknowing what we think we know.

We are not there yet, perhaps we will never arrive: so don't let me pretend I'm a guru.

'Keep it simple', says the wise guide, 'and remember, all is gift.'

nada

So as to taste the best
learn the taste of nothing

So as to own all
let go of everything

So as to become who you are
walk away from yourself

So as to become wise
forget all you ever knew

So as to arrive at where you are not
you must walk the path of a nobody

JOHN OF THE CROSS

I will take away their heart of stone
and give them hearts of flesh

Then they shall be my people
and I will be their God

EZECHIEL 11:19

John's gospel story tells again and again how people encountered Jesus and were changed by his coming into their lives. Nicodemus, the cripple lying helpless by the poolside; notably, the unsuspecting Samaritan woman coming to fetch her daily water from the village well.

Prayer too is encounter – every bit as real as that enactment beside the well. And all the elements are here. A weary Christ who has embraced the toil and hardship of human living: 'Tired after his journey, he sat down beside the well.' There is suspicion, a certain distancing, on the woman's side. She is aware that he is a Jew, she a mere Samaritan. But Jesus sweeps this aside and asks her for a drink.

The symbolism is stark: I come to prayer doubting the reality of my encounter with God, guilty of the past, borne down by my earthed humanity. Yet here is Christ, weary and thirsty, come to find me. And he asks my help ...

Jacob it was who 'wrestled' all night long with an angel. 'I will not let you go until you bless me.' The story's focus is the well that Jacob passed on to his son. To pastoral people their well is the mainstay of their wealth, where they may rely upon a continuing source of water – for their family, for their flocks.

John sees Christ as the well of a new people. 'Whoever drinks this water will still thirst again. But anyone who drinks the water I shall give will never thirst again. The water I shall give will turn into a spring within, welling up to eternal life.'

Who could resist such an offer?

'Give me this water ...'

give me this water

At noon a woman comes to the well
She is thirsty
from the heat of the day

She begins to draw water
but a Jew is sitting there
and she a Samaritan

He too is tired
from his journey

Yet this Man
seems different –
talks to her
offers to slake her thirst
he seems to know
her innermost needs

But first
she must ask
seek
open herself to his tender gaze

In that silent space
the woman
recognizes
the Man
this Man who knows her
through and through

only then she speaks
Give me this water

JOHN SKINNER

105

only in you

On first finding Julian, I knew her at once for a soul mate. Her gentle certainty about God's dealings with us: how he is courteous, intimate, ever present. Above all her vision of the Trinity lovingly at work in all our human affairs, especially in our pain and difficulties.

Here her wisdom on prayer, borne from her long experience as an anchorite, spills off the page, so that my words risk diluting her meaning. Christ comes to heal: and when thanked his reply is 'your faith has made you whole again'. His active love needs my open hands to receive, to trust that he is present and attentive.

'Cling fast to the goodness of God ...'

The touching *naïveté* of her prayer, which becomes my prayer – for its blinding simplicity invites and overwhelms.

'If I ask anything that is less I am ever left wanting ...'

And lastly, Julian brings us her vision of the active One and Three: 'our Maker, our Keeper, our Lover ... everlasting joy and bliss by our Lord Jesus Christ.'

only in you

I understood this revelation
to teach our soul to cling fast
to the goodness of God

I remembered all the different ways
we are accustomed to pray
how busy we become
when we lose sight
of how God loves us

What pleases God
what delights him most
is when we pray simply
trusting in his goodness
holding on to him
relying upon his grace

God
of your goodness
give me yourself
for you are enough to me
and I may nothing ask that is less
that may be full worship to you
And if I ask anything that is less
I am ever left wanting
but only in you
I have all

For the Trinity is God
and God is the Trinity
The Trinity is our Maker and Keeper
the Trinity is our everlasting Lover
everlasting joy and bliss
by our Lord Jesus Christ

JULIAN OF NORWICH
The First Showing

The great Psalm 139 is among the most intimate of David's songs. Sensitive to mankind's reluctance to engage with God, the psalmist is drawn into relationship in spite of himself. In his poem *The Hound of Heaven*, Francis Thompson echoes the same ambivalence: 'I fled him down the nights and down the days, I fled him down the arches of the years, I fled him down the labyrinthine ways ...'

As fast as we attempt to escape, the Hound outruns us. We turn a corner, hoping to escape, only to run right into his arms again. That is one expression of the inescapable love of our Maker. But the psalmist is still more perceptive. Like Julian, he experiences his Maker within; a loving Father who has been present from the very dawn of consciousness. For God's love precedes his creation: we were all present to him before ever we were fashioned so carefully in our mother's womb.

Faced with this mystery, I fall silent. A silence of gratitude, of recognition: a silence of peace and joy that I am among the countless members of this human family invited into the eternal Divine Presence.

I am come face to face with Love Itself: who knew Abraham, Isaac and Jacob and all who have followed in faith.

without within

When I go outside myself
I often find myself without

Yet you are everywhere without

Where could I go to escape your Loving Spirit?
If I climb to the highest heaven
you are there
present if I were to flee into the desert of despair

Father
you know me
you penetrate me
you know my innermost thoughts

If I rest within
I am no longer without
In this Silence within
I find rest in your arms

For it was you who made me through and through
this inner Self of mine
you who knitted me in my mother's womb

For all these mysteries I thank you
for this miracle that is myself
for the wonder of all you have made
for your Loving Spirit embracing me

JOHN SKINNER
(based on Psalm 139)

DECEMBER

DECEMBER

I have a dream

There is no one quite so challenging as Meister Eckhart. His originality is always bound to startle. But it is that same kind of start
we give when we are suddenly woken. Awake to reality, as I've
never before viewed it.

Pregnancy and nothingness seem opposites. But playing with
the paradox of our Maker, I suddenly see sense. For I was formed
from nothing; and I am being again-made (to use Julian's expression) in this process we experience as living. And I need to turn to
the nothingness of this second womb in order to collaborate in
this Divine working. I must join his creative initiative without
getting in the way. Remember Nicodemus and his puzzlement
when he was told, 'you must be born a second time ...' This is a
new Birth to which I am intimately related: 'from this Nothingness, He is being born'. The Son was spoken by the Father from
all eternity: now the Son of Man is giving birth to his new
creation.

A new-born needs feeding. That too is on hand. A mother
lovingly gives her breast to her baby. The Father feeds us lovingly
on his gift, 'the Bread that comes down from heaven'.

Life is given again to make the world whole once more.

The mystery that awakens us each Christmastide.

I have a dream

I have a dream

In my dream
I am pregnant
full of Nothingness
just like a pregnant mum

And from this Nothingness
He is being born

I tell you straight
it was not Moses who gave you
bread from heaven

It is my Father
who is giving you
Bread from heaven
which is real bread

For this Bread is the Father's gift
who comes down
and is giving Life
to the whole world

MEISTER ECKHART
(based on John 6:23)

The same theme is pursued here as a Carthusian Master instructs his novices. 'We are all called into communion with Him ... plunged in Christ into the life of the Holy Trinity.' Paul speaks of adoption; as we are plunged into the waters of baptism, so are we immersed in the Love Life of the Trinity. Nothing less: for with God there are no half measures.

The older I grow, the simpler this story becomes. I only half see it and that glimpsed only from time to time. That matters not. For the reality remains unfading: I may reach out to my Maker, but he has already reached deep into me, enfolding me with his Love. If I do not feel it all the while, that takes nothing away from reality: 'in this life we experience this mystery in the darkness of our faith'.

'The love of God for us is all consuming': it comes this Christmas – and each day – as his Gift. When God loves, he doesn't merely love, he gives his all, himself. This I may only receive in silence.

growing old: reaching into God

We are called into communion with Him
which means being plunged in Christ
into the life of the Holy Trinity

In this life
we experience this mystery in the darkness of faith
an inexhaustible reality
into which each day we try to enter
letting go of every image and concept
in a naked reaching into God
as He is in Himself

This is nothing spectacular
but a calm experience of radical poverty
a resting in that ultimate heart of our liberty
where we acquiesce to the fact of our creaturehood
We are nothing
absolutely everything we are is pure gift
and the act of our liberty is receptivity in trust

Humbly we can ask for the grace of love
which is the Holy Spirit
This is not a question of feeling
we are incapable of real love
as God in Christ loves us
unless the Spirit pours it forth in our hearts

This applies as much to the love of our fellow men and women
as it does to God
In this light our virtues and vices – even our sins
are of little importance

Our poverty is far more radical
and the love of God for us all consuming

A CARTHUSIAN

his Spirit is upon you

The story of Christmas, God walking among his people, was foreseen by the prophets. They were given light enough to read God's mind, trace his masterful plan and invite people to open their hearts to the news.

How hard it seems for God to speak to us and be heard. He speaks in so many different ways: and still we remain hard of hearing. Perhaps the very simplicity of his utterance defeats me. Of course, come Christmas, we understand it all. A baby born in a stable, Mary and Joseph standing by; then in come the shepherds. Let's all sing another carol.

But that is never the real story. The truth is that I myself am intimately involved in this new birth. 'His Spirit is upon you', the angel's words to Mary: she is to conceive. But he is pouring his Spirit into every human heart; and we too will conceive, if only we listen to his Word.

That is the simple story of Christmas. So simple, I might almost miss out.

his Spirit is upon you

From his wealth
we have all received
gift upon flowing gift

We were given the Law
through Moses
Spirit and Truth
have poured
through
Jesus Christ

No one
has ever seen
God
Only the Son
nearest to the Father's heart
It is he
who has made
him known

On him
the Spirit of Yahweh
rests

The Man
on whom you see the Spirit rest
is the one
who will pour his Spirit
upon you

based on ISAIAH 11; JOHN 1

117

dies natalis

I have just written my birthday card to Julia: my granddaughter will be seven in ten days' time. And we will all join in her excitement at celebrating her birthday. But which birthday are we marking? Her seventh is very important, the first great milestone, the first age of mankind. Six more to stride through. We speak of our birthday and number it accordingly. But is it not the first birthday we are celebrating: there would be no party today if Julia hadn't made it on day one.

But we none of us would be here at all were it not for that first birthday of all – the birth of Jesuah, son of Miriam. For he is the firstborn of all. As Julian tells us: 'Yet humanity's fair nature was first prepared for his own Son, the second Person: then, when the chosen time came, by full accord of all the Trinity, he made us all at once; and in our making, he knitted us and oned us to himself.'

We must never take god-words literally. God is too simple for that. Julian has her perfect way of explaining the 'trickle down' of our human generation. Jesus, even as the little new-born boy of Bethlehem, is our firstborn. For in his Son, the Father knows and loves himself; and through the Son, the Father knows and loves us – oneing us to the Trinity.

dies natalis

Father of Life
you breathe yourself
as Word

knowing
loving
in your Son

In him
you see yourself

and all
in him

Through him
all creation flows

By him
you give us Life

So that we may live
again
in your love

Father
for this I thank you
all our Ways

JOHN SKINNER

Epilogue

Together with his wife Judith, and with the blessing of the Carthusians, John conceived a simple invitation to the prayer of silence. *Hear our Silence* workshops are an opportunity for a small group to come for a day to experience and explore together the meaning of silence. House groups have resulted and there is also a circle of Friends of *Hear our Silence* who support our work and receive our monthly prayer readings together with a personal letter.

John Skinner may be contacted through Gracewing

Tom Longford
Gracewing
2 Southern Avenue
Leominster
HR6 0QF

or by email: wordman@HearourSilence.com

Lightning Source UK Ltd.
Milton Keynes UK
18 August 2009

142803UK00001B/29/P